How to Protect Yourself from Magic

Abu Ammaar

Fortress of Protection: Guarding Yourself from the Dangers of Magic

Abu Ammaar

Published by Muddassir Khan, 2024.

Table of Contents

Introduction

Magic or witchcraft is nothing but a trick of Shaytaan, and Shaytaan is a declared enemy of humanity. So, how could any of his tricks be good or beneficial for people?! That cannot happen.

Allah, glorified and exalted be He, says (interpretation of the meaning):

"O mankind!" Indeed, the promise of Allah is true. So do not let this present life deceive you, and do not let the principal deceiver (Satan) deceive you about Allah.

Surely, Shaytaan (Satan) is an enemy to you, so take him (treat him) as an enemy. He only invites his Hizb (his followers) so that they may become the inhabitants of the blazing Fire.

[Faatir 35:5-6].

Magic Definition

Magic linguistically: applies to that which the reason is unknown.

As for the terminology: The types of magic vary, and their paths are different; there is no collective definition.

Mohamed Al-Ameen Al-Shanqeedi, may Allah have mercy on him, said: "Know that magic, in terms of terminology, cannot be limited by a specific boundary or an encompassing definition that would restrict its various types, due to the abundance of different types that fall under it." There is no common measure that unifies them and serves as a restriction for the others. Thus, the expressions of scholars regarding its limits have evidently differed.

And Ibn Al-Qayyim, may Allah have mercy on him, said: "Magic is the rise of influences from malevolent souls, and the application of natural powers derived from them."

And it is possible that magic is identified by: the doors of effervescence, the suspension of objects, the tying of knots, and the actions that the magician performs after his disbelief in Allah, drawing closer to Shaytan through these actions; thus, these actions affect the one who is struck by magic with the permission of Allah.

The History of Magic

No nation has passed among the nations without Allah sending them a prophet to call them to the worship of Allah Alone, Majestic and Exalted, and He forbade them polytheism, Glorified and Exalted be He said:

And there is no nation without a warner among them. (Fatir:24) And every nation to which a messenger is sent, its people mock him, and they call him a magician, indicating the recognition of all nations with magic since their existence and their spread on Earth, and throughout history and their expansion on earth over the ages, and through the succession of generations over the centuries, Exalted be He said:

Similarly, no messenger came to those who preceded them without them saying: A magician or a madman. (Adh-Dhariyat:52) Ibn Hajar, may Allah have mercy on him, said: "And magic was present during the time of Nuh; if Allah had informed about the people of Nuh claiming: he is a magician," and he said: "The story of Harut and Marut was prior to the time of Nuh, peace be upon him, according to what has been mentioned by Ibn Ishaq and others."

And the emergence of magic spread among nations and diminished in others; for during the time of Musa (peace be upon him) , magic and magicians became popular, and they confronted Musa with their magic. Ibn Khaldun, may Allah have mercy on him, said: "And magic was in Babylon and Egypt – during the mission of Musa (peace be upon him) – deceptive markets."

Is magic a reality or an illusion?

4

Magic has a true and real existence, as it can cause a separation between spouses – by the permission of Allah – as He, Exalted be He, said:

And they learn from them what causes separation between a man and his wife. (Al-Baqarah:102)

And this has an influence on the pain of the body and its destruction through illness or death, and it can affect the well-being of the person touched by magic, all of this – by the permission of Allah – the narrator, may Allah have mercy on him, said: "Magic is a reality, and the one who is affected by magic may die, or their character and customs may change, even if they do not initiate it."

And Al-Nawawi, may Allah have mercy on him, said: "The authentic position is that magic is a reality, as we have presented." It is the consensus of the majority, and it is the opinion of scholars in general. This is attested by the well-known authentic sources of the Quran and Sunnah.

And Ibn Al-Qayyim, may Allah have mercy on him, said: ((And indeed, this has been proven by His word:

And from the evil of those who blow on knots (Al-Falaq:4) .

The dangers of magic

The most precious possession a Muslim has in this life is their religion, and the wise person is the one who protects their religion and does not accept any action that could defame, diminish, or tarnish their faith.

And magic and the seeking of sorcerers for the act of magic represent a great danger to faith; for the request of the act of magic from the magician is one of the nullifiers of Islam. Sheikh Muhammad ibn Abdul Wahhab said: The seventh - that is, the seventh nullifier of Islam - is magic, and among it are: separation and attraction, so whoever practices it, or is pleased with it, has disbelieved; and the proof is His word, Exalted be He:

But they do not teach anyone unless they say, "We are a trial, so do not disbelieve." (Al-Baqara:102) . For the magician and the pursuit of him for magic; the judgment of both is equal.

And whoever practices magic has indeed committed polytheism, the Prophet, peace and blessings be upon him, said: "And whoever casts spells; indeed, he has committed polytheism." Reported by Al-Nissaii, Al-Sheikh Abdulrahman Ibn Hassan, may Allah have mercy on him, said: ((This is a narration indicating that the magician is a polytheist)) .

And it is forbidden in all the religions of the prophets, Exalted be He said:

And the magician will not succeed, no matter where he is. (Taha:69) The Prophet (peace be upon him) said: "Avoid the seven destructive things." He was asked: "What are they, O Messenger of Allah?" He replied: Associating anyone or anything with Allah in worship; magic, killing a soul that Allah has forbidden except for a just cause, consuming usury, consuming the property of an orphan, fleeing from the battlefield, and slandering chaste, innocent, and believing women. Reported by Bukhari and Muslim.

And magic brings destruction in religion, by calling for the help of jinn and Shaytan, by hanging amulets and necklaces, by binding the heart to the fear of someone other than Allah, by rejecting trust in Allah, by corrupting people's livelihoods and their benefits, and by violating the text of jurisprudence in this regard. Exalted be He said:

And do not cause corruption on the earth after its reformation. And invoke Him with fear and hope. Indeed, the mercy of Allah is near to the doers of good (Al-A'raf:56) .

The Magician sold his religion

Indeed, the magician has sold his religion and his soul to Shaytan, for Shaytan is not satisfied with anything less than being worshipped. Exalted is He said:

But they certainly knew that whoever bought it would have no share in the Hereafter. (Al-Baqarah 102) And the magician can only practice his magic by leaving this religion – either by sacrificing to the jinn or relying on them, or by insulting the words of Allah or other things among the destructive sins. Sheikh Al-Islam, may Allah have mercy on him, said: ((They write the words of Allah with impurities – they can change the words of Allah

Majestic and Exalted is He, whether the letters of Al-Fatiha, or the letters of

Say, "He is Allah, [who is] One. (Al-Ikhlas:1) or other than that - whether it be blood or other than that, whether other than impurities, or they write other than that which pleases Shaytan or they speak by that)).

And whoever sells his soul to Shaytan has abandoned the best of character and praiseworthy actions, and he becomes blinded in vision, rushing towards evil, avoiding righteousness, opposing the religion by mocking it, angry with his family, vindictive towards his society, and he may commit, in order to please his evil soul and his tainted desires, foolish acts and association.

Sheikh Al-Islam, may Allah have mercy on him, said about them: "The end of their affair: doubt in the Merciful, the worship of Taghut and Shayateen, the commission of acts of deception, and corruption on earth. Few of them achieve their goal, which only increases their distance from Allah, and most of them are deprived and sinful. They desire disbelief, distrust, and disobedience, and they only achieve the spread of lies and wish for transgression, listeners of falsehood, devourers of what is unlawful. Upon them is the humiliation of the inventors of falsehood."

And Allah created Adam from clay, and He created the jinn from fire, Exalted is He said: (Al-Hijr 26-27) ,And Allah has favored the descendants of Adam over the jinn, Exalted is He said:

And We have certainly honored the children of Adam, carried them on land and sea, provided them with good things, and preferred them over many of those We created, with a definite preference. (Al-Isra 70) .And the magician refuses unless he humbles himself before those who are beneath him. Sheikh Al-Islam, may Allah have mercy on him, said: "And they – meaning the jinn – know that humanity is more honorable than them and of a higher rank, but if a man submits to them and seeks refuge in them; he is among the greatest of people, but if they submit to the most fallen among them so that they can fulfill his need."

Why does Shaytan serve the magician?

Shaytan is the enemy of man, he waits for him on the straight path of Allah, and he comes to him from all directions and sides, his concern is that man worships creation other than Allah.

By Your power, I will lead them all astray * Except for Your chosen servants among them (Sad:82-83) And magic is not complete for the magician except through the worship of Shaytan and leaving the religion of Islam.

But they do not teach anyone unless they say: We are a trial, so do not renounce the faith. (Al-Baqara:102) Then, when the servant abandons the religion, it is indeed Shaytan who has pushed him towards the Fire of Hell, and this is his intention in attracting the descendants of Adam. Sheikh Al-Islam, may Allah have mercy on him, said: "His goal is that a man worships a Shaytan among the Shayateen, fasts before him, prays and offers sacrifices to him, until he gains something in worldly life; his corruption is greater than his privilege, and his sin is greater than his benefit."

And Shaytan serves the magician to abuse the servants of Allah and to separate them from their wives and their possessions, to corrupt their sustenance and harm them, and to seek division and discord, Exalted is He said:

And they learn from them what causes separation between a man and his wife. (Al-Baqara:102) And he diverts them from the Lord of the worlds, so that they rely on something other than Him, on the Shayateen and their worshippers; on magicians, diviners, and fortune-tellers.

The plot of the magicians

The magicians are the servants of the Shayadeen, and the shaytaan seek their worshippers who have fallen into their polytheism: to mislead the servants of Allah, indeed the magician can command his follower to sacrifice to someone other than Allah.

And he may order him to hang polytheistic amulets on his body, or under his pillow when he sleeps, thus the magician leads his follower into polytheism. The Prophet, peace and blessings be upon him, said: "Whoever hangs an amulet has committed polytheism." Reported by Ahmed, and this is part of their plot, thus the servant falls into polytheism.

And among the plots of the magicians, they deceive anyone who comes to them with knowledge about what happens to them in terms of diseases and sufferings, for they inform them of diseases from which no one is exempt. For example, they say to them: your head sometimes hurts, or you sometimes complain about your back, or sadness and worry occasionally come to you, or you will fall into a problem and get out of it, or you will receive something that will make you happy, and so on with these general expressions and phrases that apply to everyone. Their intention behind this is to catch those who come to them in order to have authority over them.

And among their schemes: they write verses from the Quran on their magical papers; to deceive people and make them believe that they do not seek the help of jinn, but rather seek the help of Allah; in order to dupe the credulous among the people with this.

The signs of the magicians

Each magician has methods he uses for himself, in order to deceive ordinary people, and among the signs that commonly appear in many magicians, we find the following:

1. He asks the person who comes to him their name, their mother's name, and their age, and this is the most obvious sign of a magician; because he deals with the Shayadeen.

2. That he asks for remnants of what his magic needs; such as underwear, a lock of hair, or a piece of nail.

3. Ask for a photo of the person on whom he wants to cast a spell; do not give any photo to any of the servants or other people, as they could indeed use it to practice magic against you.

And this is part of the wisdom of prohibiting photography, and the fruits of committing to the ordinance of not taking photos, the Prophet, peace and blessings be upon him, said: "Allah curses those who create representations of living beings." Reported by Bukhari, do not leave any photo of yourself, your wife, or your children that is not necessary; so that you do not fall into the warnings regarding photography, the Prophet, peace and blessings be upon him, said: "Every producer of representations of living things is in Hell" (Reported by Bukhari and Muslim) .

4. Use smoke and incense, and place them in the brazier; for this attracts the Shayateen so they can carry out their actions.

5. Work during the night; and this is mainly the time for their work. Ibn Al-Qayyim, may Allah have mercy on him, said: "The domain of magic and the extent of its influence only manifest during the night, not during the day, because night magic is for them the powerful magic in influence," and if the work of magic is not done at night, the magician takes refuge in a dark place for their work.

6. Use incomprehensible words – murmurs and lip diacritics – which make it difficult for the listener to understand.

7. Combine verses from the Quran and prophetic narrations with whispers during the treatment; to deceive people into believing that he is not a magician, but that he only uses the Quran.

8. That he asks for an animal with a specific description.

9. Use the books of magicians, and those that contain symbols and occult tables, and sometimes he places them by his side if he trusts the sick person.

10. Write a talisman, or symbols, or disjointed letters, or numbers, or squares, circles, and occult tables.

11. Give the person a headpiece in the shape of a triangle or a square wrapped in leather or a piece of metal or copper, and place polytheistic invocations, numbers, and letters on it, and the magician can order him to hang it around his neck or shoulder, or place it under his pillow, and he urges him not to ignore it, and frightens him with illness or something else if he abandons it.

12. Give the sick person papers containing talismans and incense; he burns them and uses the incense.

13. Give the sick person papers containing talismans with disconnected letters, and inside there are sigil symbols and numbers, he orders them to soak them in water, then drink that water, or he commands them to wash with it.

These are therefore some signs of magicians, and these signs are also shared with soothsayers, fortune tellers, and deceptive magicians. Thus, if any of these signs appear in any of them, fear for yourself the corruption of your faith, and keep your distance from them, for indeed, whoever abandons something for the sake of Allah, Allah will compensate them with something better.

Women and the magician

He who has great intelligence keeps away from deceivers, and among women, there are those who easily succumb to fate if their wish is not fulfilled, as they strive to pursue it even if it is not in accordance with Allah's approval; thus, she seeks refuge with a magician who will deceive her and be alone with her, and he may violate her honor and order her to return to him another time, so that he can achieve his goals, and he may cast a spell on her to make her return to him, so that he can take her wealth and violate her honor.

Al-Qurtubi, may Allah have mercy on him, said: "And with whom they engage the most among people: women, especially during their menstruation," and the majority of the fuel of Hell is made up of women. The Prophet, peace and blessings be upon him, said: "I was shown Hell and that the majority of its inhabitants were women." Reported by Bukhari and Muslim.

Thus, it is incumbent upon women to fear Allah, for the fear of Allah is a source of happiness and delight, Exalted be He said:

And whoever fears Allah, He will make for him a way out and provide for him from where he does not expect. (Al-Talaq:2-3) And it is incumbent upon them to be content with destiny, and they should not exchange their religion for desires and wishes from magicians and sinful liars. And if they wish to accomplish something, they should seek refuge with Allah through supplication and persist in asking Him, Exalted is He; He is the Bestower of blessings and the Repeller of afflictions.

Exalted is He said:

And if Allah touches you with adversity, there is no remover of it except Him; and if He intends for you good, then there is no repeller of His bounty. (Surah Yunus:107)

The Oppression of the Magician

The magician, with his magic, commits various forms of transgression and oppression; how many men have been drawn by the magician towards polytheism when he ordered them to sacrifice to others besides Allah, to hang an amulet, or to believe in news of the unseen that no one knows except Allah.

And some of the magicians commit immoral acts, especially towards the women who come to them.

And the magician has corrupted many happy homes; how many loving and harmonious couples have they separated, and how many children have they turned away from their parents, tasting the bitterness of life because of him?!

How much trouble has the magician brought to people?! For how many healthy beings has he caused illness, and how many happy families have seen their union broken? And how many people in poverty carry debts and difficulties in search of the well-being that was taken from them because of an aggressive magician?

And how many others has a magician oppressed by consuming their wealth in lies; through his supposed treatment or his pretense of knowledge of the invisible?!

Indeed, the magician is malevolent towards society, and he accepts no decision except to corrupt it; thus, he is not satisfied with the happiness of others, nor with the wealth of the rich, nor with the elevation of the honorable.

Indeed, the magician is openly harmful to society, there is no goodness in him in any way, does society see the magician exercising any goodness or benefit for the people in poverty, or supporting orphans, or taking care of widows? On the contrary, his actions are solely aimed at harming society and plunging its members into polytheism, legitimizing misfortunes, afflictions, worries, and debts.

The reality of the magician

The magician is the most malevolent of people in soul, his nature is the worst among them, the most degraded in his actions, and the oppressor in his heart. Ibn Al-Qayyim, may Allah have mercy on him, said: "The magician only acts with evil souls that suit these spirits," and he also said: "Darkened hearts are the strength of the Shayateen, their home and their refuge."

The magician is the greatest fool among people, the least wise, and the most corrupt in spirit. He prefers the immediate to the hereafter in order to achieve illusory ambitions in life, and he prefers actions that he knows are destined for Hell. Ibn Al-Qayyim said: "Rarely does a magician engage without some form of worship to the Shayateen and without drawing closer to them; either by slaughtering in their name, or by a slaughter that he dedicates to them; it then becomes a slaughter for someone other than Allah, and other than that is part of the ways of polytheism and association."

The magician is close to Shaytan, similar to him in affliction towards creation. Al-Awlassi, may Allah have mercy on him, said: "The Shayateen only cooperate with wicked people who resemble them in evil and impurities in speech and belief."

The magician is described with the most despicable traits attributed to humans; lying, he lies to those who come to him with fabricated news; as the Prophet Muhammad, peace and blessings be upon him, said: "For they add lies to it, a hundred lies." Reported by Bukhari and Muslim.

The magician rises above others by the description of arrogance; and it is this description that expelled Iblis from Paradise, Exalted be He said:

Except for Iblis, he was arrogant and became among the disbelievers. (Sad:74) The magician is proud and turns his cheek with disdain towards people, and he is the most humble creation towards Shaytan and the most fearful of him, Exalted be He said:

And there were men among humanity who sought refuge with the men of the jinn, so they increased their burden. (Al-Jinn:6) For whoever humbles himself before the devil, it is his right to be humiliated and brought low in return.

Does the magician live happily?

The magician lives in misery in this life, disconnected from the happiness of life and lacking the sweetness of religion, he hates listening to the Quran and fears the call to prayer, Exalted is He said:

And whoever turns away from My remembrance - indeed, he will have a depressed life, and We will gather him on the Day of Resurrection blind. (TaHa:124) The magician spends his time away from people, he does not associate with them and only frequents them when asked to practice magic and inflict trials on people. Sheikh Al-Islam, may Allah have mercy on him, describes the state of the magician by saying: "dressed in impurities, living with dogs, he takes refuge in baths, garbage, cemeteries, and dumps, his smell is foul, he does not purify himself according to religious law, nor does he clean himself."

The magician is miserable in life; he does not sleep at night in joy, nor does he wake up in the morning in satisfaction; on the contrary, he spends his nights with smoke and demonic quotes, and polytheistic murmurs in dark places, then he sleeps during the day depressed.

This is the condition of the rebellious magician.

And your Lord is never unjust to His servants. (fusilat:46) Exalted be He said:

And as for those who have disbelieved, I will punish them with a severe punishment in this world and in the Hereafter, and they will have no helper. (Al-Imran: 56) And every action that the magician performs returns, and his state of mind is upon it and upon the one who asked him for the magic, Exalted is He said:

But the evil plot only engulfs its own people. (Fatir:43) And the magician – wherever he turns his face – is inscribed with misery and loss, Exalted be He said:

And the magician will not succeed wherever he is (TaHa:69) , Al-Gurdabi, may Allah have mercy on him, said: ((which means: he neither reaches nor is saved wherever he is on earth)) .

And the actions of the magician, all of them, will be rendered void before Allah; for his disbelief in Allah, Exalted is He, has said:

And it has already been revealed to you, as well as to those before you, that if you associate partners with Allah, your work will surely become vain. (Al-Zummar:65) .And what can be asked of one who comes to Him and is promised the Fire of Hell?! And who desires to satisfy his cunning, and he is the most despicable creation of Allah?!

What is the benefit for the magician in practicing magic?

The magician practices magic in pursuit of an illusory rank, substituting it for a lack in his soul; so that Shaytan can insult him. Sheikh Al-Islam, may Allah have mercy on him, said: "You will find those who engage in magic and invoke the stars and exalt them, they address them and prostrate before them, indeed the request of one of them is wealth and leadership, thus he denies and associates partners with Allah; for what he imagines to obtain in leadership and wealth, and he finds only what harms him and does not benefit him, as indicated by the inductive reasoning of the conditions of the world."

And the magician casts magic and falls into polytheism; hoping for wealth, when Pharaoh asked the magicians to confront Moses, peace be upon him, with magic, they asked him for wealth. Allah said, informing about the magicians, that they said:

Is there really a reward for us if we are the victors? (Shu'ura:41) , Pharaoh promised them wealth, and he also promised to bring them closer to him because the magicians love wealth and appearance.

And the magician practices magic, knowing that he becomes a slave of Shaytan, and that Shaytan has caused him much harm and corrupted many beneficial interests for him; he strives to harm others. Sheikh Al-Islam said: "And Shaytan himself is evil; if one who has determination, divisions, and magical spiritual books, and so on, draws near to him with what they love of disbelief and polytheism; it becomes like corruption and incitement for them; thus, some accomplish some of his objectives; just as one gives money to another, so that he can kill for him the one he needs to kill, or help him in immorality, or obtain immorality with him."

The reward of the magician

Due to the immense danger that magicians pose to individuals and societies, their punishment is decapitation, so that society is saved from their evils. Bijalah ibn Abduh, may Allah have mercy on him, said: "Omar Al-Khattab, may Allah be pleased with him, had written to his workers: kill every magician and sorceress." Reported by Bayhagi in the Sunan Al-Kubrah, it has been authentically reported from Hafsa, may Allah be pleased with her: "That she had ordered the execution of one of her slaves who had cast a spell on her, and thus she was executed." Reported by Malik in Al-Mowda.

And this is the reward for those who do not believe in Allah and harm the servants of Allah in this worldly life, and regarding the reward in the Hereafter; it is as the Exalted said:

But they certainly knew that whoever bought it would have no share in the Hereafter (Al-Baqarah 102) ; Meaning: he will have no share of good in the Hereafter, nor any share at all, rather his refuge is the Fire of Hell.

The pursuit of the magician

The pursuer of magic is a partner of the magician in sin.

Whoever pursues a magician for an act of magic for them; they have sold their religion for their worldly life, and have exposed themselves to the wrath of Allah by committing one of the nullifications of Islam; and it is satisfaction in magic. Sheikh

Mohamed ibn AbdulWahab, may Allah have mercy on him, said: "Whoever commits it – that is, magic – or is satisfied with it; has disbelieved."

Whoever pursues magicians to harm others has reached the peak of envy; when he has envied others because of a blessing that Allah granted him, and has corrupted his afterlife by following his desires, and by not being satisfied with what Allah has destined and decreed.

The pursuer of the magician commits a sinful error; in it are found: disobedience to the Creator and oppression of the creation.

Indeed, the one who seeks to harm others does not achieve what they desire; for Allah elevates the status of the oppressed above that of the oppressor, and the one affected by magic can achieve what they hope for. Sheikh Al-Islam, may Allah have mercy on him, said: "His hatred – that is, the envious one – for Allah's favor upon His servant is a disease; for indeed, this favor can return to the envied one and be greater, and he may find the equivalent of this favor for the equivalent of the envied one."

Beware, O oppressor, lest your magic turns against you, and may Allah not grant anyone the power to harm you through magic or otherwise.

And there is no hand except that the Hand of Allah is above it, and there is no oppressor except that he is tested by an oppressor. Exalted be He said:

The evil plot only encompasses its own people. (Fatir:43) Ibn Katheer, may Allah have mercy on him, said: ((meaning: and he will not bring misfortune upon anyone but themselves... and Muhammad ibn Ka'ab Al-Qudrabi, may Allah have mercy on him: Whoever does three things is not saved until he discharges himself of them: whoever plots secretly, transgresses, or breaks his word, and his statement is in the Book of Allah)) .

And the supplications of the one afflicted by magic are a remedy day and night, and Allah promises to respond to the supplication of the oppressed, the Prophet, peace and blessings be upon him: ((Three supplications are answered without a doubt: The supplication of the oppressed, the supplication of the traveler, and the supplication of a father for his child)) Reported by Tirmidhi.

He who plots against creation is more powerless to plot against the Creator, Exalted be He, said:

Allah is quicker in strategy. (Younis:21) And the oppressed innocents are the most important to defend, Exalted is He said:

Indeed, Allah defends those who have believed. Indeed, Allah does not love those who are treacherous and ungrateful. (Al-Hajj:38) And the result of oppression is disastrous, the oppressor is promised with a great punishment, Exalted is He said:

And whoever commits an injustice among you, We will make him taste a great punishment. (Al-Furqan:19) Indeed, the pursuer of magicians is the prey of shaytan in abandoning religion; he has forgotten that worldly life is short, and that he will rest in a dark grave alone, and that he will stand before Him, a Just Judge who will take from him for the one afflicted by magic a reward that caused his affliction by magic.

So declare your repentance, O pursuer of magicians, and untie the knot of magic from the one you have afflicted with magic before the circle turns against you.

Protection against magic

Protection against magic before it occurs

Allah created man and made enemies for him, and He legislated means to be used as protection against the evils of negative energies, and among these:

1. Trust in Allah, for the believer must attach his heart to his Lord and entrust all his affairs to Allah, and he must know that he will never be struck by an affliction except what Allah has decreed, as the Prophet, peace and blessings be upon him, said: "And know that if the nation were to gather to benefit you something, they would not be able to benefit you anything except what Allah has already prescribed for you." And if they gathered to harm you in any way, they would not harm you except with what Allah had already decreed against you. The pens have been lifted and the pages have dried. Reported by Tirmithii.

And not all magicians affect the target with magic, because how many magicians have tied the knot of magic without affecting the target with magic?! And when was there a way for the shayateen to corrupt the universe?! Exalted be He said:

But they do not harm anyone by this, except by the permission of Allah. (Al-Baqara:102)

2. Increase the remembrance of Allah, Exalted is He – through the recitation of the Quran, repentance, glorification, and other

types of remembrance – for it is the secure fortress – by the permission of Allah – against evils, and whenever people turn away from Allah and do not seek refuge with Him, and do not turn towards Him; their calamity becomes greater, and their trials increase, and they find demons among humans and jinn who are accessible.

Ibn Al-Qayyim, may Allah have mercy on him, said: "Thus, when the heart is filled with Allah, immersed in His remembrance, and guided by His directives, supplications, invocations, and seeking refuge, without deviation or inconsistency, his heart and tongue are aligned." It is one of the greatest means to prevent the influence of magic and one of the greatest remedies after being affected.

3. Avoiding sins; particularly listening to music; as it is one of the main reasons that attract Shayateen into homes and souls, and the recitation of the Quran and the remembrance of Allah drive them away.

4. Taking care to perform the Fajr prayer in congregation with Muslims in the mosques. The Prophet Muhammad, peace and blessings be upon him, said: "Whoever performs the Fajr prayer will be under the protection of Allah." Reported by Muslim, and whoever is under the protection of Allah; Shaytan has no power over him.

5. Reciting Surah Al-Baqarah in the house, the Prophet, peace and blessings be upon him, said: "Recite Surah Al-Baqarah, for taking it is a cause of blessings and abandoning it produces regrets, and the magicians cannot face it." Reported by Muslim,

and he said: "Indeed, Shaytan flees from the house in which Surah Al-Baqarah is recited." Reported by Muslim.

6. The careful maintenance of the recitation of the refuge verses during the morning and the night, and the Prophet, peace and blessings be upon him, certainly instructed Ugbah Amir, may Allah be pleased with both of them, and he said to him: "Use them when you seek refuge in Allah, for no seeker of refuge can seek refuge in anything compared to them for their purpose." Reported by Abu Dawood.

Ibn Al-Qayyim, may Allah have mercy on him, said: "The servant's need to seek refuge in Allah through these two chapters is greater than his need for his soul, his food, his drink, and his clothing."

7. Increase seeking refuge in the Perfect Words of Allah against the evil of what He has created, during the night and the morning, and at the entrance of every house – in a building, or in the desert, or in the air, or at sea – the Prophet, peace and blessings be upon him, said: "If someone descends somewhere and says: I seek refuge in the Perfect Words of Allah against the evil of what He has created; nothing will harm him until he leaves that place of descent." Reported by Muslim.

8. RECITING THE LAST two verses of Chapter Baqarah at the beginning of the night, and they are:

THE MESSENGER HAS BELIEVED in what was revealed to him by his Lord, as have the believers. All believed in Allah, His angels, His books, and His messengers. We make no distinction between any of His messengers. And they say, We hear and we obey. Your forgiveness, our Lord, and to You is the destination * Allah does not burden a soul beyond its capacity. It will have what it has earned of good, and it will bear what it has earned of evil. Our Lord, do not hold us accountable if we have forgotten or made a mistake. Our Lord, and do not impose upon us a burden like the one You imposed on those before us. Our Lord, and do not impose on us a burden that we do not have the capacity to bear. And pardon us; and grant us forgiveness; and have mercy on us. You are our protector, so grant us victory over the disbelieving people. (Al-Baqarah:285-286) The Prophet Muhammad, peace and blessings be upon him, said: "Whoever recites the last two verses of Surah Al-Baqarah at night, they will suffice him." Reported by Bukhari and Muslim.

9. Reciting Ayat Al-Kursi before sleeping, the Prophet, peace and blessings be upon him, said: "Whoever recites it when he lies down in his bed; for indeed Allah sends a guardian who will not leave him, and Shaytan will not approach him until morning." Reported by Bukhari.

10. Consuming seven Ajwa dates from Madinah in the morning – and the Ajwa date: is a type of date among the dates of Madinah – the Prophet, peace and blessings be upon him, said: "Whoever eats seven Ajwa dates for breakfast, will not be harmed that day by poison or magic." Reported by Bukhari and Muslim.

11. The careful maintenance of the mention of the morning and evening mentioned; and of this:

• a. The recitation of Ayah Al-Kursi:

———

ALLAH, THERE IS NO deity except Him, the Ever-Living, the Sustainer of existence. Neither drowsiness overtakes Him, nor sleep. To Him belongs all that is in the heavens and all that is on the earth. Who can intercede with Him except by His permission? He knows what is before them and what will be after them, and they encompass nothing of His knowledge except what He wills. His Kursi extends over the heavens and the earth, and their preservation does not tire Him. And He is the Most High, the Most Great. (Al-Baqarah:255)

b. The recitation of the two chapters of seeking refuge and they are:

———

SAY, I SEEK REFUGE with the Lord of the dawn * From the evil of what He has created * And from the evil of the darkness when it settles * And from the evil of the blowers in knots * And from the evil of an envious when he envies (Al-Falaq:1-5)

———

SAY, I SEEK REFUGE with the Lord of mankind * The Sovereign of mankind * The God of mankind * From the evil of the whisperer who withdraws * Who whispers in the breasts of mankind * Among jinn and men (Al-Nas:1-6)

C. SAY: "IN THE NAME of Allah, the One with whose name nothing can cause harm on earth or in the heavens, and He is the All-Hearing, the All-Knowing" three times, the Prophet, peace and blessings be upon him, said: "Whoever recites: In the name of Allah, the One with whose name nothing can cause harm on earth or in the heavens, and He is the All-Hearing, the All-Knowing - three times - will not be struck by a calamity until he wakes up in the morning, and whoever recites it when he wakes up in the morning - three times - will not be struck by a calamity until he goes to sleep." Reported by Abu Dawood.

· D. SAY: ((I SEEK refuge in the Perfect Words of Allah from the evil of what He has created)) Reported by Abu Huraira, may Allah be pleased with him, who said: ((A man came to the Prophet, peace and blessings be upon him, and said: O Prophet of Allah, I was stung by a scorpion last night! He replied: Rather, if you had said: I seek refuge in the Perfect Words of Allah from the evil of what He has created, it would not have harmed you. Reported by Muslim.

E. BY SAYING: "I SEEK refuge in the Perfect Words of Allah, which neither the righteous nor the corrupt can overcome, against the evil of what He has created, of what He has made, and of what He has scattered, against the evil of what descends from the heavens, and what ascends to them, against the evil of what He has scattered on earth, and what emerges from it, against the trials of the day and night, and against the evil of every nocturnal visitor, except the nocturnal visitor who comes with good. O Most Merciful One." Reported by Ahmed.

F. THE SAYING: "ALLAH is sufficient for me." There is no deity worthy of worship but Him. I have placed my trust in Him, He is the Lord of the Majestic Throne)) – seven times -, reported by Abu Al-Dara' may Allah be pleased with him, who said: ((If someone says upon waking or falling asleep: Allah is sufficient for me. There is no other deity worthy of worship but Him. I have entrusted my trust to Him, He is the Lord of the Majestic Throne – seven times –, Allah will suffice him against all that grieves him, whether he is honest in reciting them or a liar)) Reported by Abu Dawood.

· G. ABU BAKR, MAY Allah be pleased with him, said: O Messenger of Allah, teach me something that I can say when I wake up in the morning and when I go to sleep at night. He said: Say: O Allah, Knower of the unseen and the seen, Creator of the heavens and the earth - Lord and Sovereign of all things, I bear witness that there is no deity worthy of worship except You; I seek refuge with You from the evil of myself and from the evil of Shaytan and the polytheism to which he calls people, he said: to say it morning and evening, and when he goes to bed)) Reported by Al-Tirmidhi.

· h. Say: ((There is no deity worthy of worship except Allah, alone, without any partner. The Kingdom and praise belong to Him, and He has power over all things)) , and the Prophet, peace and blessings be upon him, said: ((And whoever says: There is no deity worthy of worship except Allah, alone, without partner. The Kingdom and praise belong to Him, and He has power over all things - one hundred times a day -; it is the same for him as freeing ten slaves, and one hundred good deeds are written for him and one hundred sins are erased from him, and it is a protection against Shaytan for that day until the evening when he goes to sleep, and no one will surpass him in performing better good deeds except for the one who recites these words more often than that.

Reported by Bukhari and Muslim.

And the neglect of the mentioned morning and evening invocations is one of the main reasons for Shaytan's domination over man, and one of the reasons for the affliction of the evil eye. Ibn Al-Qayyim, may Allah have mercy on him, said: "And the majority of the domination of the evil soul over its owners – that is, the seizures – is due to the diminishment of their religion, and the corruption of their hearts and tongues in relation to the reality of invocation and the seeking of refuge and fortification based on prophecy and faith."

The method of reciting the mentioned remembrance for children and women

The morning and evening remembrance is a supplication that fortifies the individual against the evils of men and jinn, and it is not necessary to spit dryly while reading the mentioned remembrance, just as the presence of your child or your wife near you is not a condition when you recite the mentioned remembrance and the fortification for them; for the mentioned remembrances are supplications, imploring your Lord to protect them, and there is no condition to spit dryly or to be in their presence.

And the way to recite the mentioned supplication for your children, your spouse, or anyone among your relatives, or others, is as follows:

Say:

1. I SEEK REFUGE FOR you with the Lord of the Dawn, against the evil of what He has created, and against the evil of the darkness when it settles, and against the evil of the blowers in knots, and against the evil of an envious one when he envies.

· 2. I SEEK REFUGE for you with the Lord of mankind, the Sovereign of mankind, the God of mankind, against the evil of the whisperer who withdraws, who whispers in the breasts of mankind, among jinn and men.

3. I seek refuge for both of you in the perfect words of Allah, against every devil and every poisonous thing, and against the evil eye that influences; for indeed, the Prophet, peace and blessings be upon him, used to seek refuge with this supplication for Al-Hassan and Al-Hussein, may Allah be pleased with them both. Reported by Al-Bukhari.

4. I SEEK REFUGE FOR you in the Perfect Words of Allah against the evil of what He has created – three times – and so on for the other supplications.

Those Who Are Affected by Magic

He who is close to Allah is distant from evils and misfortunes, and those who are close to their Lord are those who increase His remembrance in fortification, preventing the evils of the Shayateen upon men and jinn. Exalted is He said:

Indeed, over My servants, you have no authority. And your Lord is sufficient as a Disposer of affairs (Al-Isra:65) , and if the servant abandons the remembrance of Allah or His worship, the protection of his Protector diminishes; it will then be easier for Shaytan to take possession of him.

And the impact of magic is on the hearts that are mostly empty of the worship of Allah and His remembrance. Ibn Al-Qayyim, may Allah have mercy on him, said: "It primarily affects – that is, magic – women, children, the ignorant, the Bedouins, and those who have diminished their share of religion, trust in Allah, and Tawhid, and those who have no share of the divinely mentioned remembrance, supplications, and seeking prophetic refuge."

Women are among those most affected by magic; due to their diminished worship and remembrance of Allah, as well as children; due to the negligence of parents and guardians in reciting the mentioned remembrance over them, and likewise the people of immorality, disobedience, and mischief.

And among those most affected by magic or the evil eye are those who fill their homes with musical instruments; for magic and the evil eye are inherently malevolent, and whoever distances themselves from the Most Merciful and draws closer to disobedience will be more easily impacted, unlike those who seek protection from Allah and whose hearts are filled with His remembrance; indeed, Shaytan fears those in this state. Exalted is He, He informed regarding Iblis:

He said: By Your power, I will surely lead them astray, except for Your chosen servants among them. (Sad:82-83) The method of removing magic

How is magic cast?

Magic is practiced in different ways, and here are the methods that are followed:

· 1. Magic is cast by consuming food, when the magic is cast on the food, and it is consumed by the person targeted by the magic without their knowledge; thus, the magic is inflicted upon them – with the permission of Allah – and it may not be inflicted with the permission of Allah.

· 2. Magic is cast through drink; because the person targeted by the magic has consumed juice or tea or something of that sort.

Magic in food or drink is cast with a mucilaginous material that adheres to the abdominal wall; so that the magic remains in the stomach of the person affected by the magic, and if the person targeted by the magic does not treat this type of magic through emesis; otherwise, their stomach will be harmed.

3. Magic is cast by sprinkling, that is, by placing the magic on a patch of ground, because if the person targeted by the magic steps on it, they will be affected – with Allah's permission – and it may not cause harm thanks to Allah's protection over the servant.

· 4. Magic is practiced through writing; using talismans and magical symbols without needing any remains of the targeted person, and this is – by the will of Allah – its influence on the person affected by the magic is weak; otherwise, there must be remains of the targeted person.

5. Magic is practiced through knots; this is done by taking a remnant from the target of the magic – such as hair or a piece of clothing – then a knot will be made by a tailor, and afterwards, he will spit on it dryly with his evil soul.

And the Prophet, peace and blessings be upon him, was a victim of this type of magic with a comb and hairpins – that is, the remnants of hair – then the magic was placed on them, afterwards the magic was hidden in the dry spathe of the date palm, and then it was thrown into the well, as reported by Sahih Bukhari and Muslim.

The way to know where the magic was cast

The place where the magic is cast is known in two ways according to Islamic law:

1. Either the jinn who guards the magic pronounces it in the body of the one struck by the magic after reading the Quran over them, then informs of the location of the magic; afterwards, it is removed.

2. Or Allah grants His favor to the one who is a victim of magic by sending them a dream indicating its location; so that they may know its location through the dream.

Two reasons for the removal of magic

1. The devoted supplication to Allah to remove magic, Aisha may Allah be pleased with her said: ((The Messenger of Allah, peace and blessings be upon him, used to imagine that he had done something, even if he had not done it, until one morning – or; one night – the Messenger of Allah, peace and blessings be upon him, invoked Allah, then he invoked again, and again he invoked...)) Reported by Muslim and Bukhari; then Allah answered his supplication.

The state of supplication rests upon insistence and commitment to the manners of supplication; such as facing the qibla and observing the moments of response like the last third of the night; for indeed Allah says during this time: "Who will call upon Me so that I may respond?" And who will ask for forgiveness from Me so that I may forgive him? Reported by Muslim and Bukhari, and the Prophet, peace and blessings be upon him, said: "Indeed, there is an hour in the night when no Muslim asks Allah for anything good regarding worldly life or the Hereafter, without Allah granting it to him, and this is every night." Reported by Muslim.

2. Commit to seeking forgiveness and increasing its practice; for indeed, it is one of the greatest reasons for alleviating distress, Exalted is He said:

And He said, Seek forgiveness from your Lord. Indeed, He is always a perpetual Forgiver * He will send down upon you the heavens in showers * And He will give you an increase in wealth and children and provide for you gardens and provide for you rivers (Nuh 10-12) Verses to read for people affected by magic

Allah has made the great Quran a healing for diseases, and every verse of Allah's verses has a healing, and there are verses that impact – with Allah's permission – those affected by magic, and among these:

1. Surah Al-Fatiha, which is the greatest chapter of the Book of Allah, reported by Bukhari.

· 2. Ayah Al-Kursi, which is the greatest verse of the Book of Allah, reported by Muslim.

Ibn Al-Qayyim, may Allah be pleased with him, said: "And he – that is, Sheikh Al-Islam – used to treat with Ayah Al-Kursi, and he would instruct those afflicted by convulsions to increase its recitation and anyone who treated them to do the same, as well as to read the two chapters seeking refuge."

3. The end of Surah Al-Baqarah; ((Whoever recites the last two verses of Surah Al-Baqarah in one night, it is sufficient for him)) .

· 4. Verses of magic mentioned in the chapter Al-A'raf, and it is the word of Allah, Exalted be He:

And We inspired Moses: Throw down your staff, and it immediately devoured what they had falsified. Thus, the truth was established, and what they were doing was abolished. They were defeated on the spot and became humiliated (Al-A'raf:117-119) .

5. The verses from Surah Yunus, and it is the word of Allah, Exalted be He:

And Pharaoh said: Bring me every knowledgeable magician. So, when the magicians arrived, Moses said to them: Throw down what you are going to throw. And when they had thrown down, Moses said: What you have brought is magic. Indeed, Allah will expose its futility * Indeed, Allah does not correct the work of the corruptors * And Allah will establish the truth by His words, even if the criminals hate it (Yunis:79-82)

6. The verses from Chapter Taha, and this is the word of Allah, Exalted be He:

They said, "O Moses, either you throw first or we will be the first to throw." He said, "Rather, you throw." And suddenly, their ropes and sticks appeared to him, because of their magic, as if they were moving. And he felt apprehension within himself, said Moses. We [that is, Allah] said: "Do not be afraid." Indeed, it is you who are superior. And throw down what is in your right hand; it will swallow up what they have made. What they have fabricated is only the trick of a magician, and the magician will not succeed wherever he is. (Taha:65-69)

7. Reciting the two refuge supplications, Aisha, may Allah be pleased with her, said: "When the Prophet, peace and blessings be upon him, complained, he would recite the refuge invocations over himself and lightly spit, and when his pain increased, I would recite over him and rub him with his hand,

hoping to receive blessings from it." Reported by Bukhari and Muslim.

Ibn Katheer, may Allah have mercy on him, said: "The most beneficial use for the elimination of magic is what Allah revealed to His Messenger, peace and blessings be upon him, to eliminate it; and these are the two chapters of seeking refuge, and in the narration: 'There is no better seeking of refuge than the chapters of seeking refuge,' and also the recitation of Ayat al-Kursi, for it drives away the devils."

Seeking protection through supplications and seeking refuge through Islamic legislation

There are supplications and prophetic methods to seek refuge in the quest for protection; among them:

· 1. ((O ALLAH, LORD of the people! Remove the misfortune and heal the patient, for You are the Healer. No healing is useful except Yours; a healing that will leave no illness. Reported by Bukhari and Muslim.

---

2. THE SEEKING OF PROTECTION that Jibreel, peace be upon him, performed on the Prophet, peace and blessings be upon him, and this is his narration: ((In the name of Allah, I recite a prayer over you, against the evil of every person and the evil eye. In the name of Allah, I recite a prayer over you, may Allah heal you. Reported by Muslim.

---

3. THE SUPPLICATION said for the sick, the Prophet, peace and blessings be upon him, said: "There is no Muslim servant who visits a sick person - except at the time of death - and says seven times: 'I ask Allah the Magnificent, Lord of the

Magnificent Throne, to heal you,' except that he will be healed."
Reported by Ahmed.

The method to remove magic

Magic has many types, and for each type, there is a specific method to resolve it. The explanation for this is as follows.

First: If the magic has been consumed through food or drink, how to resolve it is:

By eliminating it from the stomach through the process of excretion or vomiting.

How to resolve it from the stomach as follows:

· 1. Present half a kilo of senna from Mecca.

· 2. Take the amount of two cups of water, place it in a kettle.

· 3. Take two handfuls of senna leaves and place them in the kettle.

· 4. By placing the kettle filled with senna leaves and water on the fire, let it boil for about three minutes.

· 5. When you wake up during Fajr; drink two cups of it cold.

· 6. After drinking two cups, walk for about fifteen minutes.

· 7. Do not eat if you drink senna; for four hours; so that the senna can take effect.

· 8. If you have drunk senna; you will feel a stomach ache, and this is common; so that senna can produce its effect.

• 9. Whoever has drunk senna; because it is necessary to go to the bathroom for the waste to pass on the first and second day, even if they are not affected by magic.

• 10. If the stomach pain persists until the third and fourth day; because this is one of the signs of the presence of magic in the stomach.

• 11. Continue drinking senna for seven days according to the method mentioned above.

• 12. If the pain persists in the stomach after a week, then drink senna for another week.

• 13. If the pain disappears and the constant need to excrete disappears; for this is a sign of the removal of magic by the permission of Allah.

And by this method, the magic that was cast through consumption or drinking is removed by the permission of Allah.

Secondly: if the magic is cast on a piece of paper; to resolve it:

Soak the paper on which the magic is written in a container of water until the remnants of the writing have disappeared, then after that, disintegrate this paper and get rid of it even if remnants of the writing still appear, and recite over the water to seek protection.

Thirdly: if the magic is cast through knots – that is: in hair or a tied thread – to resolve it, you must:

Untie these threads, so if you analyze them all, then cut the threads into pieces, and then throw them anywhere.

Fourth: If the magic is cast by being sprinkled on the ground; to resolve it, here is how to proceed:

· 1. Take a cup filled with water, then read over it: Al-Fatiha, and the verse of the Kursi and the two chapters of seeking refuge.

· 2. Sprinkle this water on the place where the magic was cast,

3. Repeat this method three times, and with Allah's permission, the magic will be lifted.

Ibn Al-Qayyim, may Allah have mercy on him, said: "It has been reported about him – that is, the Prophet, peace and blessings be upon him – regarding – that is, in the treatment of magic – by two methods:"

The first of them – and it is the most complete of them – is its elimination and annulment, just as it has been authentically reported from him, peace and blessings be upon him, that he asked this from his Lord, Exalted be He, and He guided him...

And the second method: vomiting at the place where the evil of the magic is tied.

It is not permissible to remove the magic from a magician.

It is not permissible to remove magic by a magician, whether through magic or without magic, for several reasons:

• 1. Visiting the magician is never permitted, even if it is for something other than the removal of magic, so what can be said if the visit is for the removal of magic?!

2. That the magician relies on the Shayateen to remove the magic, and this is disbelief.

Ibn Al-Qayyim, may Allah be pleased with him, said regarding the removal of magic by the forbidden method: "The removal of magic is done by casting a similar magic, and this is part of the actions of Shaytan, so the one who casts and the one who receives become close to Shaytan for what he loves."

3. The magician is pure evil; he only releases magic by lying to the person affected by the magic, or by deceiving them to take their money, and he may also violate the honor of the person affected by the magic.

The One Affected by Magic

The One Affected by Magic is Oppressed

If the servant is sincere towards his Lord; Allah, Majestic and Exalted is He, may test him by making enemies among men and shayateen, Exalted is He said

And thus, We have made for every prophet an enemy - demons among men and jinn, inspiring one another with ornamental speech in delusion (Al-An'am:112) And thus is the fate of the prophets who have gone through trials with what they have endured, and if Allah wants to elevate a servant, He tests him, the Prophet, peace and blessings be upon him, said: "Whomever Allah wants good for, He afflicts him with trials." Reported by Bukhari.

And do not be sad – O you who are afflicted by magic – about what has been inflicted upon you by the harm of magic; for the Prophet of Allah, peace and blessings be upon him, was afflicted by magic, and Allah tests His believing servant in order to bring him closer to Him. Ibn Al-Qayyim, may Allah have mercy on him, said: "He, Exalted and Majestic is He, is with the one afflicted by illness with His mercy towards him, and with kindness to bring him closer to Him, due to the pain of the heart caused by the illness; He is with the broken-hearted."

And do not be angry with what has befallen you, and do not panic at what Allah has decreed for you; for it may be the reason for your elevation, Exalted and Majestic is He said:

But perhaps you hate a thing and it is good for you; and perhaps you love a thing and it is bad for you. (Al-Baqarah:216) And if something of the opportunities of this worldly life eludes you; know then that with Allah there is something better and more lasting for those who believe and put their trust in their Lord. Sheikh Al-Islam, may Allah have mercy on him, said: "The oppressed, the envious, if he is patient and fears Allah; well-being will be for him."

So increase in saying:

Indeed, we belong to Allah, and to Him we shall return. (Al-Baqarah:156) . O Allah, reward me in my calamity, and exchange it for me with something better. Umm Salamah, may Allah be pleased with her, said: "I heard the Prophet of Allah, peace and blessings be upon him, say: If a Muslim who suffers a calamity says what Allah has commanded him, 'Indeed, we belong to Allah and indeed, to Him we will return; O Allah, reward me for my affliction and exchange it for me with something better,' Allah will exchange for him something better." When Abu Salama died, she said: Which Muslim is better than Abu Salama, whose family was the first to emigrate to the Messenger of Allah, peace and blessings be upon him. I then uttered the words, and Allah gave me in exchange the Messenger of Allah, peace and blessings be upon him. Reported by Muslim.

And the worry of worldly life, even if it closely surrounds the Muslim; for his wealth is destined to cease, even if it is prolonged, it will be replaced by a lasting pleasure in which the servant will forget all the anguish that has been taken from him. The Prophet, peace and blessings be upon him, said: "The

Messenger of Allah, peace and blessings be upon him, said, among the inhabitants of Hell, a person who led the most luxurious life in this world will be brought on the Day of Resurrection and plunged into the Fire, and he will be asked: O son of Adam!" Have you ever experienced any comfort? Have you had the chance to obtain luxury? He will respond: By Allah, no, my Lord. And then, one of the people of Jannah who had experienced extreme misery in this world will be immersed in Jannah. Then he will be asked: O son of Adam! Have you ever experienced hardship? Have you ever encountered difficulties? He will say: "By Allah, no my Lord, I have neither known misery nor gone through hardship." Reported by Muslim.

And know with certainty that the wrongdoer who pursues the magicians, responsible for your affliction through magic, will not escape from Allah, indeed your Lord is observing, Exalted is He said:

And We have never been unaware of the creation (Al-Mu'minun:17) And advance – O you who are affected by magic – towards your Lord, and being oppressed is better for you than coming to Him and being oppressed.

So, seek refuge in Allah and increase your requests for forgiveness and your supplications; for the relief from Allah is near, and beware of despairing of Allah's relief, and do not cease to take the means to remove magic through supplication and permissible remedies, and do not yield to the evils and their supporters; for the plot of the shayateen is weak, and Allah is the protector of the believers, and the disbelievers have no protector for them. Exalted be He said:

It is because Allah is the protector of those who have believed and because the disbelievers have no protector. (Muhammad:11) And Allah, exalted be He, is attributed with Power and Strength, and whatever action the oppressor executes; for Allah is above him and He grants a respite until He seizes him and does not let him go, exalted be He has said:

And never think that Allah is unaware of what the unjust do. (Ibraheem:42)

The seer

Who is the seer?

The soothsayer is: the one who claims to know what will happen in the future, so he claims – for example – that he knows when someone will die. And whether so-and-so will live happily or not, and similar matters concerning the future.

And this soothsayer claims something that neither angels nor prophets know; for no one knows the knowledge of the unseen except Allah, Exalted is He, who said:

Say: No one in the heavens and on the earth knows the unseen except Allah, and they do not perceive when they will be resurrected. (Al-Naml:65) And Majestic and Exalted is He, He said of Himself:

Knower of the unseen and the seen, the Almighty, the Wise (At-Taghabun:18) And the horoscopes they claim to know are a type of divination.

The reality of the soothsayer

The Prophet, peace and blessings be upon him, informed about the reality of soothsayers with concise and powerful words when he was asked about them; he said, "They are nothing." Reported by Bukhari and Muslim.

Sheikh Al-Islam, may Allah have mercy on him, said: ((...Just like the astrologer, the magician, and their likes, for they possess ignorance, misguidance, deception, and cunning that can only be enumerated by the Majestic One)) .

For all the keys to the unseen are in the hands of the Almighty, and people know the lies of the astrologers and their lack of truth; but the weakness of faith and the domination of Shaytan lead them to disobey Allah. Sheikh Al-Islam, may Allah have mercy on him, said: "Individuals and the general public have known through experience and recurrence that the judgments made by astrologers are that the lies are multiplied many times compared to the truth."

The tricks of the soothsayers

For the fortune teller, there are many tricks, and they apply them to those who visit them; in order to reveal to them that they know the unseen, and among their tricks:

If someone comes to them asking for information about future matters, they announce to them summarized things that happen to everyone, for example, they say: a troubling concern will come to you, then it will be lifted. They use this trick because they know that worry does not last in humans; it is rather alleviated by the mercy of Allah.

Or they tell him: You will receive provisions in the future; for they know that Allah has taken charge of providing for the wealth of every creation.

Or they tell him: Soon, you will hear news that will make you happy in your life; for they know that the essence of life is: happiness, sadness, worry, and relief.

And similar general matters that are spread to those who are unaware of their true intentions.

The lies of the diviner

The Prophet, peace and blessings be upon him, informed that the soothsayer lies in a single piece of information, adding a hundred lies, just as the Prophet, peace and blessings be upon him, said: "Until the last of them transmits it to the magician or the soothsayer... where he adds a hundred lies to that word." Reported by Bukhari and Muslim.

And if you have a companion who lies about information, even five lies, then you should abandon him and avoid his company; for he has taken your mind lightly with the abundant lies he gives you, so what about the soothsayer who lies a hundred lies and not just five lies?! Isn't it more meritorious to separate from him, to avoid him, and to distance oneself from his actions?

The proof of their lies

If the soothsayer knows the unseen as he claims, he would have prevented the evils that befell him, and if he knew the unseen, he would have known the moment of his death and repented for his disbelief towards his Lord before his soul was taken, so as not to be eternally in Hell.

And if the jinn are those who claim to provide them with knowledge of the unseen and they did not know of the death of Solomon, peace be upon him, except after a creature of the earth had eaten his staff; then how would they know? Exalted is He, He said:

And when We decreed his death, nothing indicated to them his death except a creature of the earth eating his staff. But when he fell, it became clear to the jinn that if they had known the unseen, they would not have remained in a humiliating punishment. (Saba:14)

THE CONFESSION OF A soothsayer in front of Sheikh Al-Islam Ibn Taymiyyah

No matter how much a liar exaggerates with their lies, their situation will be revealed even if it takes some time. The Prophet, peace and blessings be upon him, said: "Truthfulness is tranquility, but lying is doubt." Reported by Tirmidhi.

And the fortune-teller claims to share with Allah His knowledge of the unseen, and the Messenger of Allah, peace and blessings be upon him, informed that whoever claims to possess something they do not have, Allah will immediately expose them. The Prophet, peace and blessings be upon him, said: "Whoever boasts about receiving what they have not received is like someone who wears two garments of lies." Reported by Bukhari and Muslim.

And there was a soothsayer who confessed, during the time of Sheikh Al-Islam Ibn Taymiyyah, his lies to the people. Sheikh Al-Islam, may Allah have mercy on him, said: "This is the state of the fool, even when I spoke to them in Damascus and their leaders were present with me, and I explained the corruption of their actions with a logical reasoning that they accept as valid, a leader among them said to me: By Allah, we tell a hundred lies; when we say one true word."

If the soothsayer was accustomed to confessing not just one lie but rather to lying excessively and continuing in that lie; then why visit them, when a person finds in them nothing but the invention of falsehoods, conjectures, and claims that they associate with Allah in this?

The ruling on visiting soothsayers

The soothsayer invents lies about Allah by claiming to have an association with the Majestic and Exalted Lord in the knowledge of the unseen: thus, a severe warning came to him, and the proof of this is as follows:

1. Whoever visits a fortune teller and believes them, then they have disbelieved, and among this is palmistry and similar practices. The Prophet Muhammad, peace and blessings be upon him, said: "Whoever visits a fortune teller or a soothsayer and believes what they say, then indeed, they have disbelieved in what was revealed to Muhammad, peace and blessings be upon him." Reported by Al-Hakam.

2. And whoever visits a fortune teller solely for comfort and not to ask a forbidden, impermissible question, Ma'wiyyah ibn Al-Hakam Al-Sulami, may Allah be pleased with him, said: ((O Messenger of Allah, we were recently in a state of ignorance, then Allah brought Islam, and among us, there are men who consult fortune tellers; he (peace and blessings of Allah be upon him) said: Do not consult them)) Reported by Muslim.

Fortunetellers

Who is the seer?

The fortune teller is: the one who claims to know the things hidden from sight, claims – for example – to know what is behind the wall, and what so-and-so – for example – is doing in this specific case while being in another country..., and so on.

The judgment on visiting fortune tellers

A severe warning has been given against disbelief to anyone who consults a fortune teller; and the proof of this is as follows:

1. Whoever visits a soothsayer and believes him has certainly disbelieved, for the Messenger of Allah, peace and blessings be upon him, certainly said: "Whoever visits a soothsayer or a fortune-teller and believes what he says, has indeed disbelieved in what was revealed to Muhammad, peace and blessings be upon him." Reported by Al-Hakam.

2. Whoever visits a fortune teller just to ask a question and does not believe him; his prayer will not be accepted for forty nights, ((Whoever visits a fortune teller and asks him anything, his prayers will not be accepted for forty nights)) Reported by Muslim.

The Astrologer, the Practitioner of Abacomancy, the Practitioner of Psephomancy, the Palmists, and the Practitioner of Tasseomancy

Who are the Astrologer, the Practicer of Abacomancy, the Practicer of Psephomancy, the Palmists, and the Practicer of Tasseomancy?

The astrologer: he is the one who takes the accounts of the stars as a means to access his forbidden goal.

The practitioner of abacomancy: is the one who writes on the ground with sand; claiming to know the invisible.

the practitioner of psephomancy: is the one who throws pebbles on other pebbles and makes them roll; claiming to know the knowledge of the invisible through this.

Palmists and the practitioner of tasseography: it is the one who murmurs over the palms of men and the cups with incomprehensible pronunciations; claiming to know the knowledge of the future, and they are liars in this regard.

For the astrologer and the practitioner of abacomancy, the practitioner of psephomancy, and the palmists; are diviners or fortune tellers, and sometimes the fraudulent magician performs these actions by imitating the diviner and the fortune teller, pretending to be a diviner or a fortune teller; so that he can consume the wealth of people through deceit.

The Swindler Magician

Who is the Con Artist Magician?

The fraudulent magician: he is the one who claims to be a magician or a seer, and he lies about it.

His intention is to take people's wealth by lying to them, claiming that he practices magic, or that he heals through magic, or that he knows the future, and this is not the case. He does not succeed in this action either, but he imitates their actions and mimics their actions.

And it is not permissible to visit the fraudulent magician; he is a lying man.

The difference between the magician, the soothsayer, the seer, and the fraudulent magician

The magician: practices magic; it has an impact – by the permission of Allah – on the one who is affected by the magic.

As for the soothsayer: he claims to know what will happen in the future; as if he were informing that so-and-so will die in two months...and so on.

The seer: claims to know the unknown aspects of reality through sight and not matters of the future; as if he were informing that so-and-so – at this moment – is in his car and that he is in another country, and he does not claim to know matters of the future.

As for the fraudulent magician: he is a liar and does not know magic, divination, or clairvoyance, but he only pretends to know them; in order to consume people's wealth through lies, and his actions are popularized among naive people.

An invitation to repentance

WHOEVER APPROACHES soothsayers, or knocks on the doors of magicians, and whose soul has incited them to harm others; they must renounce these sins that corrupt religion, and they must regret the destructive sins they have committed, and never return to these miserable and shameful actions, and remove the evil by dispelling the magic on those they have affected, and draw closer to Allah through sincere repentance with a great sense of guilt, and increase their repentance and seeking of forgiveness, and voluntary acts of worship, and righteous actions, Exalted is He. He said:

But in truth, I am the Ever-Pardoning of anyone who repents, believes, does good deeds, and then continues in guidance. (Taha: 82) And when the magicians of Pharaoh repented and believed in their Lord, Allah accepted their repentance and elevated their ranks, and they became part of the followers of Moses, peace be upon him.

So follow the paths of those who repent, and beware of the ways of the wretched; the magicians and the deceptive magicians.

We ask Allah to protect Muslims from the acts of corrupt magicians, to relieve the distress of those affected by magic, and to grant them a greater good than their calamity.

May Allah grant His peace and blessings upon our Prophet Muhammad, as well as upon his family and his companions, collectively.

Conclusion

Islam strongly prohibits consulting magicians or sorcerers, as such practices contradict the principles of Tawheed (the oneness of Allah) . Seeking help from magicians is associated with shirk (polytheism) and opens the door to exploitation, deception, and harm.

MAGICIANS, CLAIMING supernatural powers or knowledge of the unseen, often manipulate their clients. Vulnerable individuals, especially women, who approach them for solutions to personal problems may become victims of abuse, including sexual assault or financial exploitation. Islam emphasizes safeguarding one's dignity and avoiding situations that can lead to harm.

Documented Cases

Several real-life incidents highlight the dangers of consulting magicians:

1. Sexual Exploitation Under the Guise of Healing

In countries like Egypt, Pakistan, and India, there have been numerous reported cases where so-called faith healers or magicians assaulted women. For example:

○ In 2020, a self-proclaimed healer in Pakistan was arrested for sexually assaulting women who sought his help. He convinced them that physical contact was necessary to "remove evil spirits."

○ A 2017 case in India involved a magician who assaulted women under the pretense of performing rituals to reunite them with estranged spouses.

2. Fraud and Abuse

In a high-profile case in Morocco, a fake healer was arrested for exploiting women financially and sexually. He used fear of curses and black magic to coerce his victims into compliance.

3. Global Patterns

Reports from various countries, including Indonesia and Sudan, document magicians taking advantage of women seeking solutions for marital or familial issues. These cases underline the risks of being alone with such individuals, who often operate outside legal or moral boundaries.

Islamic Perspective

The Quran and Hadith explicitly warn against practices involving magic and the reliance on magicians:

- **Quran (Al-Baqarah 2:102)** : Magic is condemned as a form of misguidance that leads people away from Allah.

- **Hadith:** The Prophet Muhammad (peace be upon him) said, "Whoever goes to a soothsayer or fortune-teller and believes what he says has disbelieved in what was revealed to Muhammad" (Sunan Abu Dawood, Hadith 3904) .

Muslim women should seek lawful solutions to their problems through du'a (supplication) , consultation with trusted scholars, and reliance on permissible means. Family and community support play a crucial role in avoiding the pitfalls of relying on magicians.

By adhering to Islamic teachings and seeking help through appropriate channels, one can avoid harm and protect their faith, dignity, and safety.

References and translations from As-Siḥr; Khaṭaruhu, At-Taḥaṣṣun Minhu, Kayfiyyat Ḥallihi written by Dr. Abdul Muhsin bin Muhammad Al-Qasim, Imam and Deliverer of Sermons at the Prophet's Noble Mosque and Head of the Department at the Court of Appeals in Medina.